Set Sail For Summer

Grade 2 Review

By Elizabeth Flikkema

Cover Illustration by
Dan Sharp

Inside Illustrations by
Shauna Mooney Kawasaki

Carson-Dellosa Publishing Company, Inc.
Greensboro, North Carolina

Hands-on Activity Calendar

June

These activities were designed for a child to do with an adult or older child. Some of the activities may be a review, while others will offer new information or new experiences. Have fun!

1 Each day this summer, read the date on a calendar. Learn to spell the days of the week and the months of the year.

2 Measure how tall you are and how much you weigh today. Write down the measurements on your calendar. Measure yourself again on the last day of August.

3 Start a summer journal in a spiral notebook. Write down your thoughts every day.

4 Keep a log of all the books you read this summer. Read every day. With the help of your parents, set a goal for yourself of how many books (or minutes) you think you should read each day.

5 Using exactly five toothpicks, make a design in which each toothpick touches at least one other. How many different designs can you make with five toothpicks? Copy your designs on paper. Give each one a name. Write a number sentence to describe each design.

6 Make a summer reading paper chain. Write one book title on each link as you read. How long do you think your chain will get this summer?

7 Make a puppet show of a book you have read. Write a script using the plot and some of the dialogue from the book.

8 Go to story time at your local library or bookstore.

9 Design a treasure hunt with a map and a surprise at the end. Ask a friend to find the treasure using your map.

10 How many words can you make from the letters in the phrase "outdoor fun"? Write the words in your journal.

11 Learn American Sign Language. Each day, teach yourself a new letter or word and review what you learned on previous days.

12 Make fruit smoothies with fresh fruit and yogurt in the blender. Write the recipe in your journal.

13 Play restaurant. Make a menu with all the foods you will serve and their prices. Use play money and a cash register.

14 Make a design using exactly six blocks. How many different designs can you make with six blocks? Copy your designs on paper. Give each one a name. Write a number sentence to describe each design.

© Carson-Dellosa   CD-0264 *Set Sail for Summer*

June

15 Create a "musical instrument" that makes at least two different tones. Play it for a friend.

16 Ask someone to trace your shadow on the sidewalk with chalk in the morning. Stand with your feet in the same place at noon and have someone trace again. Stand with your feet in the same place three hours later and have someone trace your shadow again. How does your shadow change throughout the day? Why does it change?

17 Dance and sing along to music in your bedroom.

18 Build a tower with blocks. Draw a picture of your tower. Use a ruler to make your drawing to scale.

19 Color dry pasta with food coloring and rubbing alcohol. Put 2 tsp. (10 mL) rubbing alcohol in a zippered plastic bag. Add several drops of food coloring and about 2 cups ($1/2$ L) pasta or rice. Use a different bag for each color. Spread wet pasta on layers of newspaper to dry. Use the pasta in art projects and to make jewelry.

20 Make a boat out of modeling clay. Float it in the sink. How many identical blocks do you think you can put in the boat before it will sink? Test your prediction.

21 Make a sand castle.

22 How many words can you make from the letters in the phrase "summer solstice"?

23 Use a ruler to measure several things around your house. Record your measurements on a piece of paper.

24 Paint a terra-cotta flowerpot with patterns and designs.

25 Make a paper airplane. Make changes to the airplane to make it fly better. Read a book about airplanes to learn how they are able to fly.

26 Count to 60 by 3s.

27 Do a blind taste-test. Ask someone to feed you foods with sweet, sour, bitter, and salty tastes. Hold your nose and close your eyes while you taste. Can you guess what the foods are?

28 Make flash cards with addition and subtraction facts. How fast can you answer all of the cards? Time yourself again on the last day of summer vacation.

29 Sort your stuffed animals or other toys into groups that make sense. Are there some toys that fit into more than one group? Make a Venn diagram to sort them again.

30 Make a job jar. Think of things that you can do in your room or house. Write them on small pieces of paper and put them in a jar. Take one out when you need something to do.

CD-0264 *Set Sail for Summer* © Carson-Dellosa

Hands-on Activity Calendar

July

1 On a large piece of paper, draw a circle, square, rectangle, diamond, triangle, and heart so that the shapes overlap and fill the page. Color the shapes with crayons using different colors and textures.

2 How many jumping jacks can you do? Find out. Practice every week. Test yourself again during the last week of August.

3 Draw and color a flag.

4 How many words can you make from the letters in the phrase "July fireworks"? Write the words in your journal.

5 Estimate and then weigh a whole watermelon. Save some of the watermelon seeds to sprout and plant in soil.

6 Ask someone to measure and pour $1/2$ cup ($1/8$ L) water into a glass and add drops of food coloring. Measure the same amount of water and pour into a second glass. Try to match the color of the water in the first glass.

7 Visit the fire station. Make a lift-the-flap book about firefighters.

8 Make paper dolls or puppets out of craft foam (can be purchased at most craft stores). Cut the people or animal shapes out of one color and make their clothes or features out of other colors.

9 Play tic-tac-toe. Write down your strategy for winning.

10 Make a design using exactly eight toy building bricks. How many different designs can you make? Copy your designs on paper. Give each one a name. Write a number sentence to describe each design.

11 Make a list of things that are heavier than a bicycle. Make a list of things that are lighter than a bicycle.

12 Think of a way to make money this summer. Get your parents to approve your plan before you start.

13 Design an obstacle course to go through on foot or on bike.

14 Make a snack mix. In a resealable plastic bag, mix together equal amounts of some or all of the following ingredients: dry cereal, peanuts, raisins, pretzels, chocolate chips, marshmallows, and crackers.

15 Estimate how much water you use each day. Measure how much water you use to wash your hands by plugging the drain before you begin. Think of ways you can save water.

© Carson-Dellosa   CD-0264 *Set Sail for Summer*

July

16 Find an ant hill and count how many ants you see around it. What do you observe about the ants?

17 Learn the names of the states or provinces around you.

18 Make an animal mask out of a paper plate.

19 Write the names of the people in your family in alphabetical order. Is there another way to organize the names?

20 Read an Arthur book by Marc Brown. Draw a picture of Arthur showing his adventures or how he helped someone in the book. Write a sentence explaining your picture.

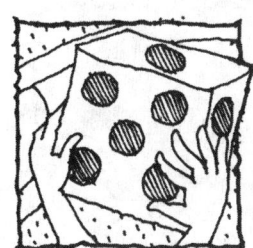

21 Use a water-soluble ink stamp pad and a felt-tip pen to make fingerprint animals. Draw legs, eyes, ears, antennae, and other parts to make ants, bunnies, frogs, spiders, and other animals.

22 Take a picture of something that is important to you. Write about your picture when it is developed.

23 Make a giant die out of a box. Draw a game board on the sidewalk with chalk. Roll the die and move yourself around the game board.

24 Pick a room in your house that has a clock. Keep a piece of paper in there and write down the time each time you walk into that room. Predict how many times you will write the time today. At the end of the day, count how many times you wrote the time.

25 Make a list of all the "communities" to which you belong (family, scouts, etc.). Number the communities in order of size.

26 Make a graph of favorite ball games. Ask friends, family, and neighbors to tell you what game with a ball they like best. Graph the results.

27 Write a list of words that have almost the same meaning as "small."

28 Dream up different races or relays that you can do with some friends. Try hopping, walking like a crab, or walking backwards. Use a stopwatch to time each race. Create ribbons or prizes for all the participants.

29 Write a story about the funniest thing that has happened so far this summer. Write the story in your journal.

30 Make a book called "All about Me." Include information about and pictures of yourself. Write about all your favorites: books, friends, toys, sports, animals, etc.

31 Look up a new word in the dictionary and learn how to spell it by heart.

Hands-on Activity Calendar

August

1 Predict which day this month will be the hottest. Write it on the calendar. Record the temperature at the same time each day.

2 Use fabric paint to decorate a T-shirt with summer words and pictures.

3 Make a list of things you can smell and a list of things you can taste. Circle the things that can go in both lists. Put the words in a Venn diagram.

4 Think of the best and worst things that happened yesterday or today.

5 What would you bring to the beach for a day? Draw a picture of yourself at the beach. Label all the things you brought with you.

6 Find a new place to read a book. Lie down under your bed with a flashlight or sit under a tree or on top of the washing machine. Crawl in a box or make a fort with sofa cushions.

7 Go to the library and check out a book about an animal. Read the book and then write about what you learned.

8 Make a frozen banana snack. Peel a banana and roll it in melted chocolate chips. Roll in chopped nuts before freezing on a paper plate.

9 Make a design using exactly 10 blocks. How many different designs can you make with 10 blocks? Copy your designs on paper. Give each one a name. Write a number sentence to describe each design.

10 Write a tongue twister, a sentence in which all (or most of) the words begin with the same letter. Ask a friend to read it three times in a row as fast as he can.

11 Make a list of words that rhyme with "wet," "game," and "run."

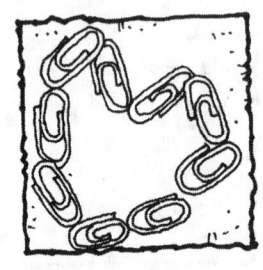

12 Read several limericks. Then, try writing your own.

13 Write as many words as you can using the letters in the phrase "ice-cream cone." Write the words in your journal.

14 Using exactly nine paper clips, make a design in which each paper clip touches at least one other. How many different designs can you make with nine paper clips? Copy your designs on paper. Give each one a name. Write a number sentence to describe each design.

15 Make a mailbox out of an empty tissue box. Write letters to people and ask them to write back. Use stickers for stamps. Ask your parents for junk mail that you can pretend to deliver.

© Carson-Dellosa 6 CD-0264 *Set Sail for Summer*

August

16 Count to 60 by 4s. How fast can you do it?

17 Go for a walk and choose something to count, such as houses with green roofs, pine trees, barking dogs, or cracks in the sidewalk.

18 Paint a picture using paint and a marble, feather, or other textured object instead of a brush.

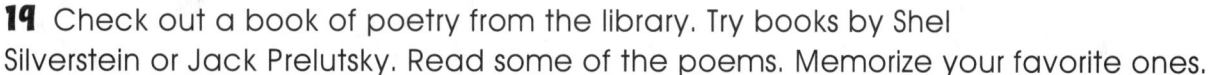

19 Check out a book of poetry from the library. Try books by Shel Silverstein or Jack Prelutsky. Read some of the poems. Memorize your favorite ones.

20 When you are watching TV today, decide what the commercials are trying to sell you.

21 Think of some questions you have that begin with "I wonder." Try to discover the answers.

22 Make a graph of the clothes and toys in your closet.

23 Write 10 different math sentences that all have an answer of 15.

24 Make a stained-glass butterfly. Cut out a large butterfly shape from black paper. Cut shapes out of the butterfly, leaving the outline. Glue colored tissue paper behind the shapes to create colorful wings.

25 Think about your favorite animal at the zoo. Write a poem about the animal in five lines. In line one, name the animal. In line two, write two words that describe the animal. In line three, write three words that describe the animal's actions. In line four, write a four-word sentence about the animal. In line five, write one word that is a synonym for the word in line one.

26 Write about what you hope to learn in third grade. Put the note away until next summer when you can read it again and compare with what you really did learn.

27 Write a list of words that sound good to you. Keep adding to your list.

28 Cut a hole in a large paper plate. Hang the plate from a tree branch with string. (Tape pennies around the bottom of the plate to hold it steady.) Throw a ball or a rolled-up sock through the hole for one point. To earn more points, stand farther away from the target.

29 Look around your home for examples of simple machines: wedges, inclined planes, levers, wheels and axles, screws, and pulleys. How many can you find? Which type of machine did you find the most?

30 Put a wide-mouth jar upside down over a grassy spot in direct sunlight. Leave the jar outside for at least one hour. What do you see inside the jar? Why?

31 Measure how tall you are and how much you weigh today. Write down the measurements and compare with those you took on the second day of June.

CD-0264 Set Sail for Summer © Carson-Dellosa

The Three Bears

story elements

Read the story. Then, answer the questions.

Once upon a time there were three bears. They lived in a large castle in a land far, far away. The baby bear was lonely because he lived so far away from all the other animals. He didn't have anyone to play with.

One morning the bears made pancakes with honey for breakfast. The bears were very hungry, but the pancakes were too hot to eat right away. They decided to walk down to the stream while their pancakes cooled.

While they were gone, a little boy who lived in a cottage in the woods knocked on the castle door. He was looking for someone to be his friend. When no one answered the door, he walked right in. He saw the plates of pancakes. Since he was a polite boy, he sat down to wait for an invitation.

Soon the bears came home. They were surprised to see the boy in their home, but bears that live in castles know all about fairy tales. They offered to share their pancakes, and the boy stayed for breakfast.

The boy told the bears that he was looking for a friend. The baby bear said, "That is exactly what I was looking for!" The boy happily came back to the castle to play with the baby bear every day ever after.

1. Who are the characters in the story? _____

2. What is the setting? (where and when) _____

3. What is the small problem the bears solve by going for a walk?

   _____

4. What is the main problem in the story? _____

5. How is the problem solved? _____

6. How is the story like a fairy tale? _____

© Carson-Dellosa

8

CD-0264 Set Sail for Summer

What's Next?

predicting outcomes

Circle the sentence that tells what will happen next.

1. Alicia packed her backpack with books and her lunch.
    a. She will go to the beach.
    b. She will go to school.
    c. She will go camping.

2. Kim found her paints, a brush, and a piece of paper.
    a. She will paint a picture.
    b. She will paint the wall.
    c. She will brush her hair.

3. After dinner, Malik took his telescope outside.
    a. He will go to bed.
    b. He will play football.
    c. He will look at stars.

4. When Madeline showed up, Mom and Dad put on their coats. They told her they would be home by 9:00.
    a. Madeline will baby-sit.
    b. Madeline will sleep overnight.
    c. Madeline will go to a movie.

5. At the store, Jesse picked out some candy that cost $1. He looked in his pocket. He had 90 cents.
    a. Jesse will buy the candy.
    b. Jesse will pick out some different candy.
    c. Jesse will eat the candy.

6. Tony woke up at 8:50. He is supposed to be at the pool by 9:00.
    a. Tony will hurry to get ready.
    b. Tony will go back to sleep.
    c. Tony will eat breakfast.

CD-0264 *Set Sail for Summer* © Carson-Dellosa

Insects

vocabulary

Read about insects.

What is black and hairy with red eyes and six legs?

I don't know, but it's crawling up your back! EEEEK!

What are insects? Most people call them bugs, but *insect* is the proper name of the largest group of animals in the world. Insects deserve our respect. All insects have six legs, two antennae, and three body parts. But insects can look as different as an ant, a grasshopper, or a butterfly. They can hop, swim, fly, or crawl. They eat a variety of foods and live in almost every habitat in the world.

Some insects are very beautiful. A butterfly usually has colorful wings. It flies gently around pretty flowers. A butterfly sips nectar from flowers. While it is eating, it helps pollinate the flowers so more flowers can grow.

Some insects are helpful. Ladybugs are a gardener's best friend. Some gardeners will even buy ladybugs and put them in their gardens to eat harmful aphids. Aphids are tiny insects that eat or kill plants. Ladybugs love to eat aphids. Do you think ladybugs like gardeners as much as gardeners like ladybugs?

Some insects seem a little nasty. Mosquitoes buzz in our ears and leave itchy reminders of their bites. They need to sip a little of our blood in order to lay their eggs. A praying mantis preys upon other insects for its lunch. It rubs its front legs together as if to pray before eating its food.

The great variety of insects in the world makes them very interesting animals to study. Discover for yourself by observing insects and reading more about them!

Insects (continued)

vocabulary

Read the clues about insects to complete the crossword puzzle.

Across
2. A beautiful insect
7. Insects have two of these
8. What mosquitoes sip
9. Number of legs an insect has

Down
1. What butterflies sip
3. Number of body parts an insect has
4. A helpful insect
5. Homonym of "prays"
6. A nasty insect

Word Box

| mantis | preys | blood | three | six |
| ladybug | nectar | antennae | butterfly |

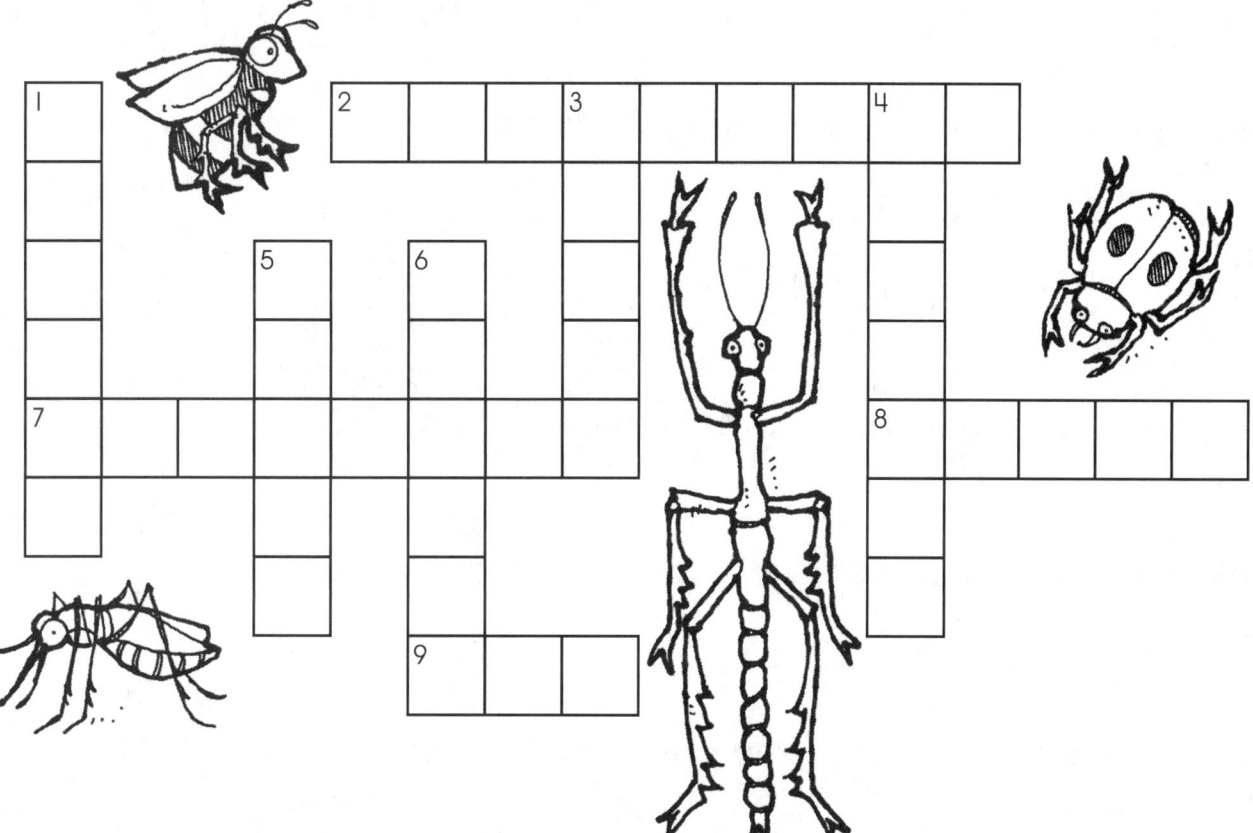

Camping Trip

reading for details/compare and contrast

Francisco and Ben are packing for a camping trip. Look at the items they have gathered and read their lists. Circle the items on each list that the boys forgot to pack.

Francisco's List

pajamas	2 pairs of jeans
shoes	4 pairs of socks
toothbrush	sleeping bag
pillow	sweatshirt
3 T-shirts	book

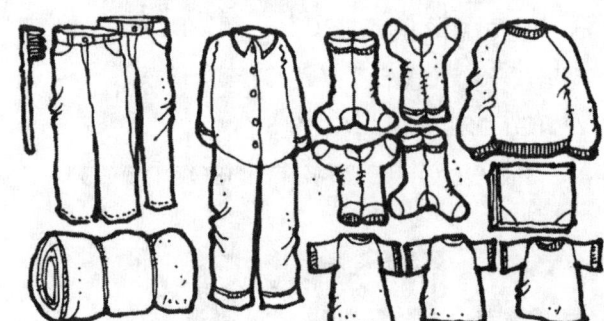

Ben's List

2 pairs of shorts	shoes
4 pairs of socks	toothbrush
toothpaste	sleeping bag
pillow	sweatshirt
4 T-shirts	radio

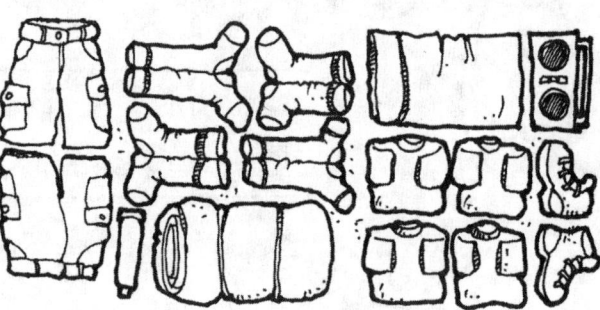

1. What items did both boys have on their lists?

   _____

2. What items were on Francisco's list but not on Ben's?

   _____

3. What items were on Ben's list but not on Francisco's?

   _____

4. What item did each boy bring to use as entertainment?

   Francisco: _____   Ben: _____

Challenge: Put the items from the boy's lists in a Venn diagram. Draw the diagram on another sheet of paper.

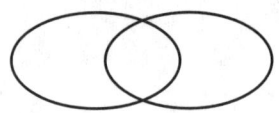

Alphabet Adventure

creative writing

Read the alphabet adventure.

One hot summer day, the letters of the alphabet were walking in the woods. They were busy talking and making different sounds. Suddenly, A fell into a ditch. A was ANGRY. He was so active and antsy, but he could not get out of the ditch. Soon the other letters heard A and came to help.

B was BRAVE and offered to climb into the ditch and give A a boost. C was CAREFUL and cautioned that B might get caught in the ditch, too. The letters took a rest so they could think of a way to help A.

D got up and DANCED with delight. She declared that E and F would make an EXCELLENT ladder together. "FANTASTIC!" said G. It was a GREAT idea. H offered to HELP, too. I helped lower the ladder INTO the ditch while J and K JUMPED with excitement like KANGAROOS. A climbed easily up the ladder to the top. L LAUGHED to see such a sight.

The letters continued on their walk. They watched M and N to MONITOR what might happen NEXT . . . .

ABCDEFGHIJKLMN

Continue the alphabet adventure. Use the letters as characters in order from M to Z to describe and solve another problem. Also include words that start with the same letters as the characters.

_____
_____
_____
_____
_____

ABC Ice Cream

alphabetical order

The ABC Ice Cream Shoppe has lots of flavors. The flavors are usually in alphabetical order, but today they are all mixed up. Put each group of flavors back in order by writing the numbers 1–4 on the lines.

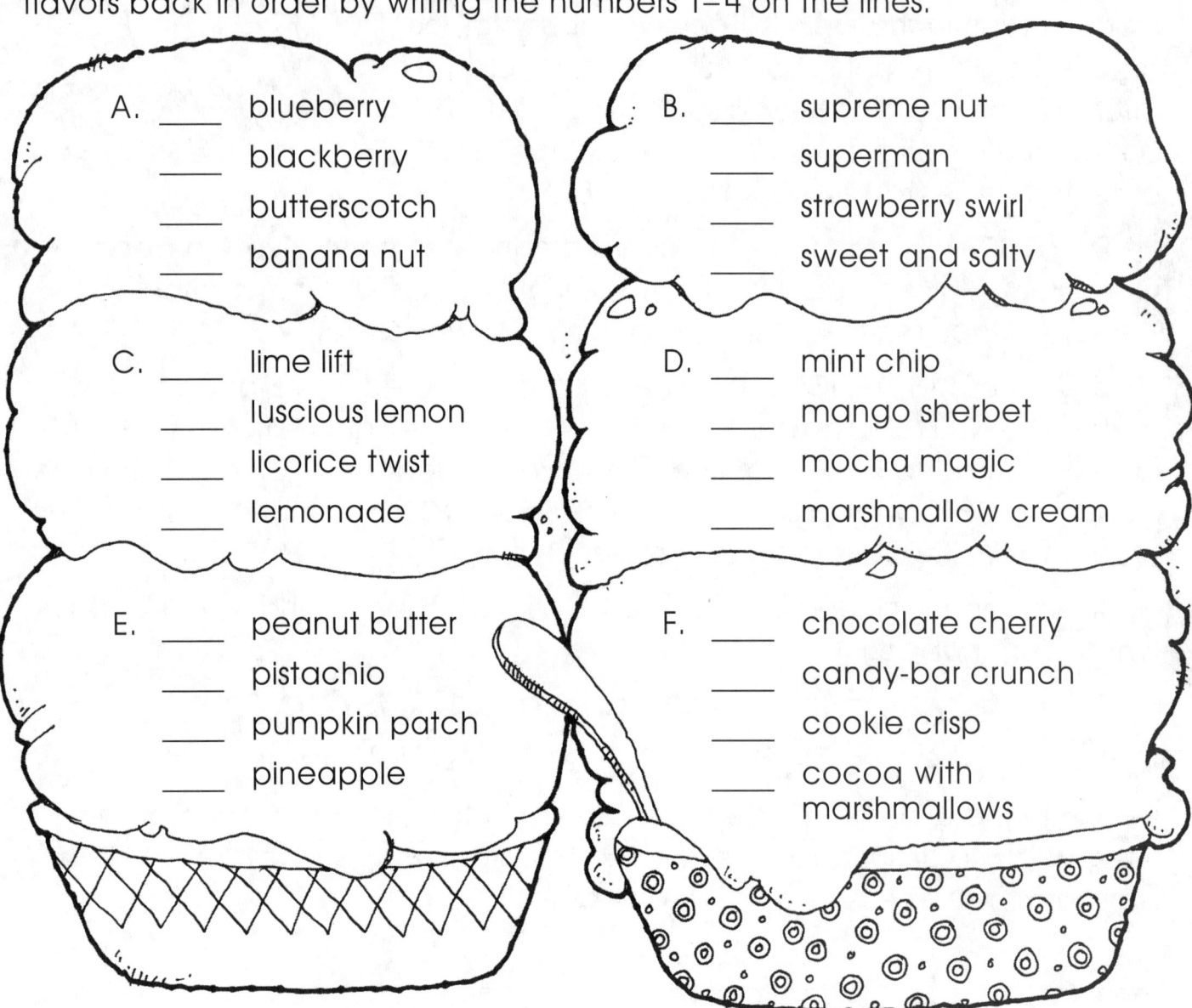

A. ___ blueberry
___ blackberry
___ butterscotch
___ banana nut

B. ___ supreme nut
___ superman
___ strawberry swirl
___ sweet and salty

C. ___ lime lift
___ luscious lemon
___ licorice twist
___ lemonade

D. ___ mint chip
___ mango sherbet
___ mocha magic
___ marshmallow cream

E. ___ peanut butter
___ pistachio
___ pumpkin patch
___ pineapple

F. ___ chocolate cherry
___ candy-bar crunch
___ cookie crisp
___ cocoa with marshmallows

Write your own creative new ice-cream flavors.

_____

Challenge: How many double-dip combinations can you make with vanilla, chocolate, and strawberry? Draw them on another sheet of paper.

Summer Analogies

critical thinking

Draw a picture to complete each analogy.

1.  is to  as  is to  .

2.  is to  as  is to  .

3.  is to  as  is to  .

4.  is to  as  is to  .

5.  is to  as  is to  .

6.  is to  as  is to  .

7.  is to  as  is to  .

8.  is to  as  is to  .

CD-0264 *Set Sail for Summer* © Carson-Dellosa

Phoebe's Vacation

contractions

Where are Phoebe and her family going on vacation this summer? To find out, follow the path of correct contractions. Circle the five incorrect contractions and write the correct forms below.

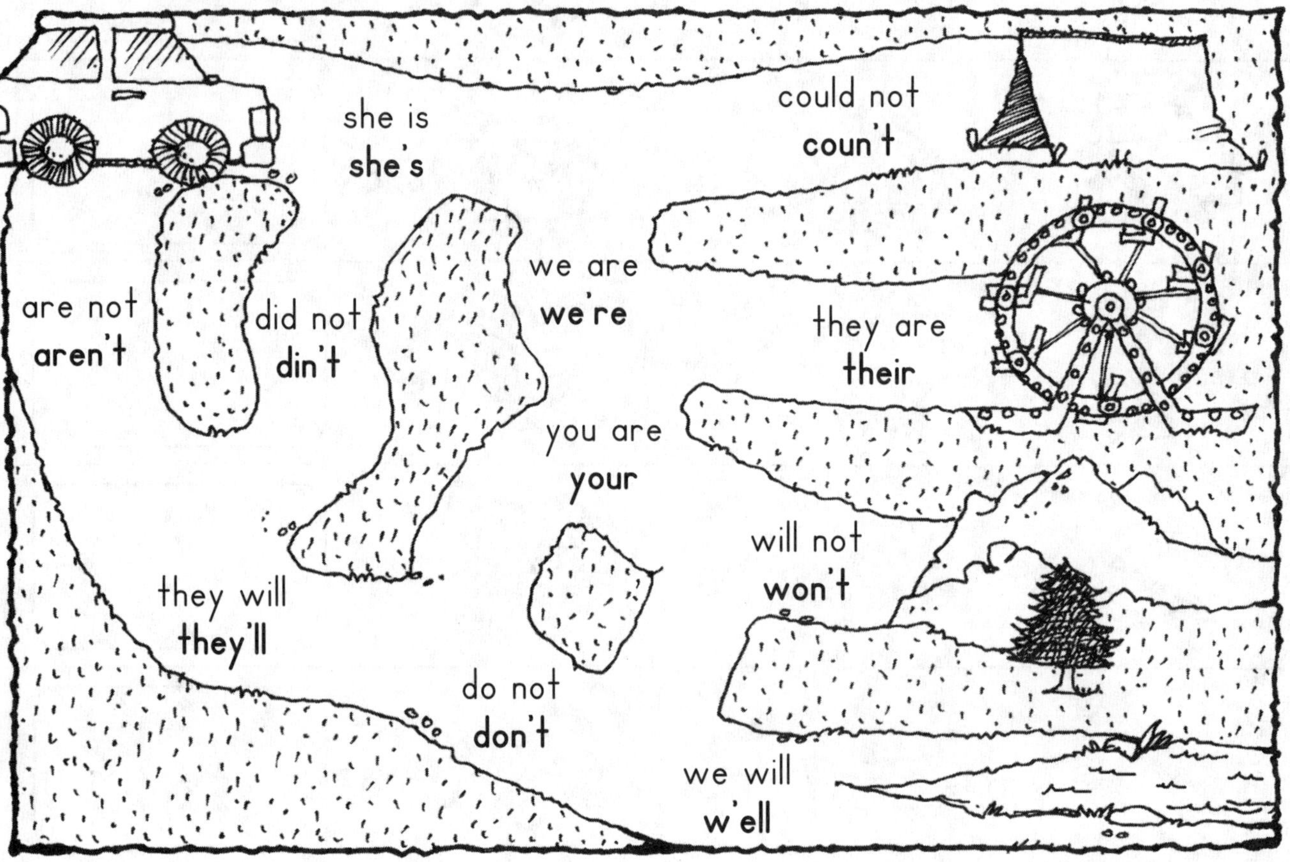

she is — **she's**	could not — **coun't**
are not — **aren't**	we are — **we're**
did not — **din't**	they are — **their**
you are — **your**	will not — **won't**
they will — **they'll**	
do not — **don't**	
we will — **w'ell**	

What is the correct path? Circle where Phoebe is going on vacation.

Fix the incorrect contractions from the maze.

1. _____ + _____ becomes _____
2. _____ + _____ becomes _____
3. _____ + _____ becomes _____
4. _____ + _____ becomes _____
5. _____ + _____ becomes _____

© Carson-Dellosa   16   CD-0264 *Set Sail for Summer*

Park Play

following directions

Read carefully and follow the directions.

1. Draw two swings on the swingset.
2. Count the squirrels and color them brown. How many? _____
3. Circle the animals that do not belong at the park.
4. What is wrong with the child on the slide?

   _____

5. Draw and color a blue-green pond in the park.
6. Color the flowers red and yellow.
7. Draw one bird in a bush.
8. Draw six apples in a tree.
9. Color each child with different colored clothes.

Beach Bash

synonyms and antonyms

Suzie sells synonyms at the seashore for seven cents. Write a synonym for the word in each shell. Synonyms are words that have the same meaning.

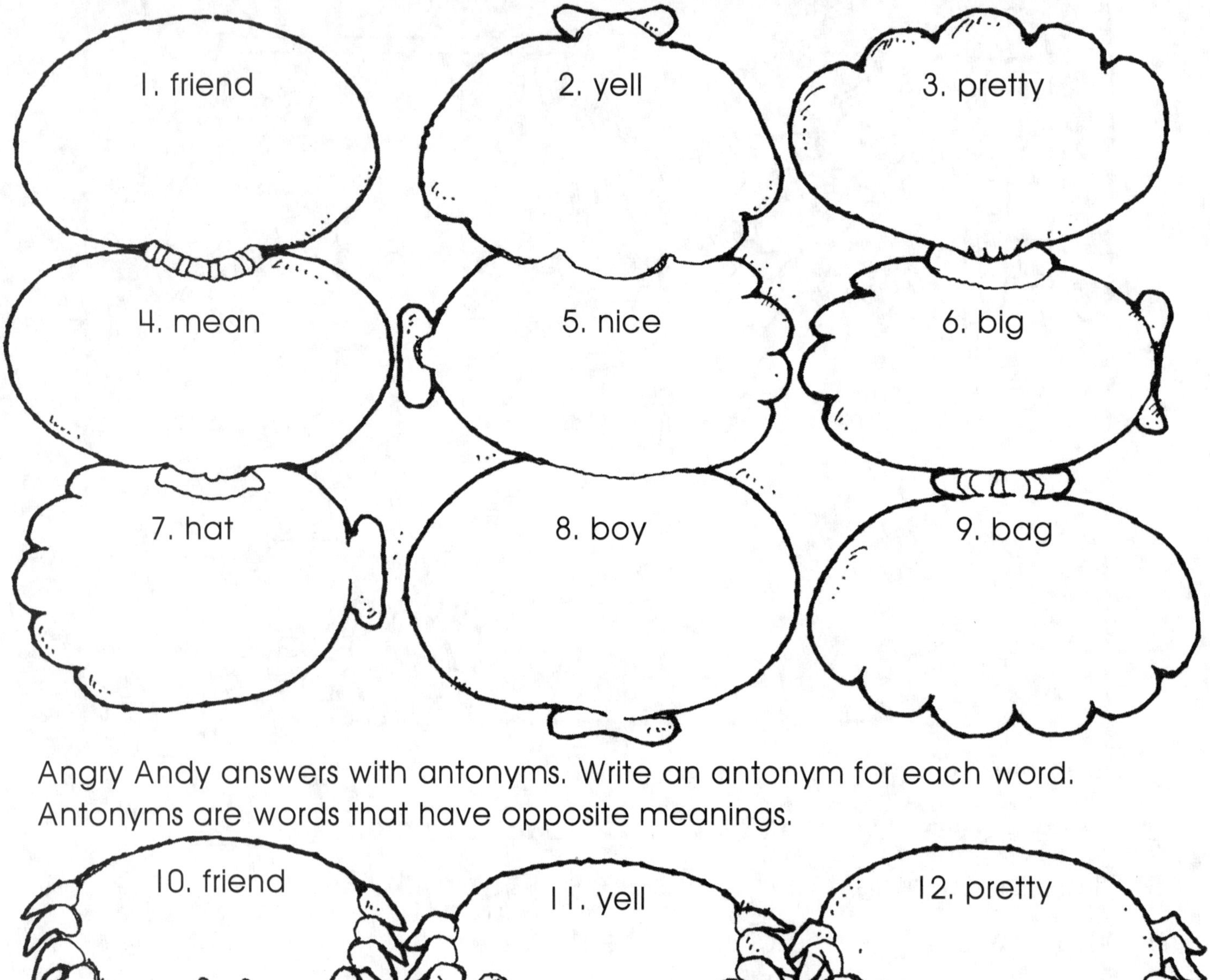

1. friend
2. yell
3. pretty
4. mean
5. nice
6. big
7. hat
8. boy
9. bag

Angry Andy answers with antonyms. Write an antonym for each word. Antonyms are words that have opposite meanings.

10. friend
11. yell
12. pretty
13. mean
14. big
15. boy

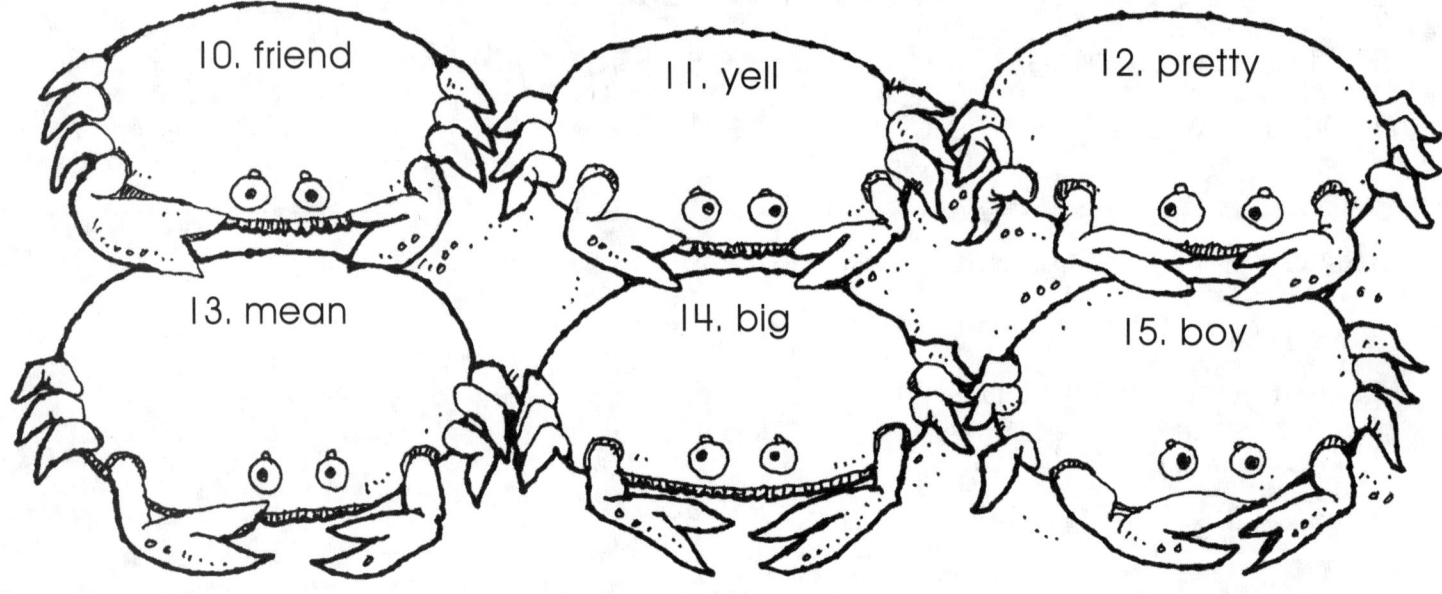

© Carson-Dellosa

18

CD-0264 *Set Sail for Summer*

Summer Sailing

skip counting

Count by 2s to connect the dots.

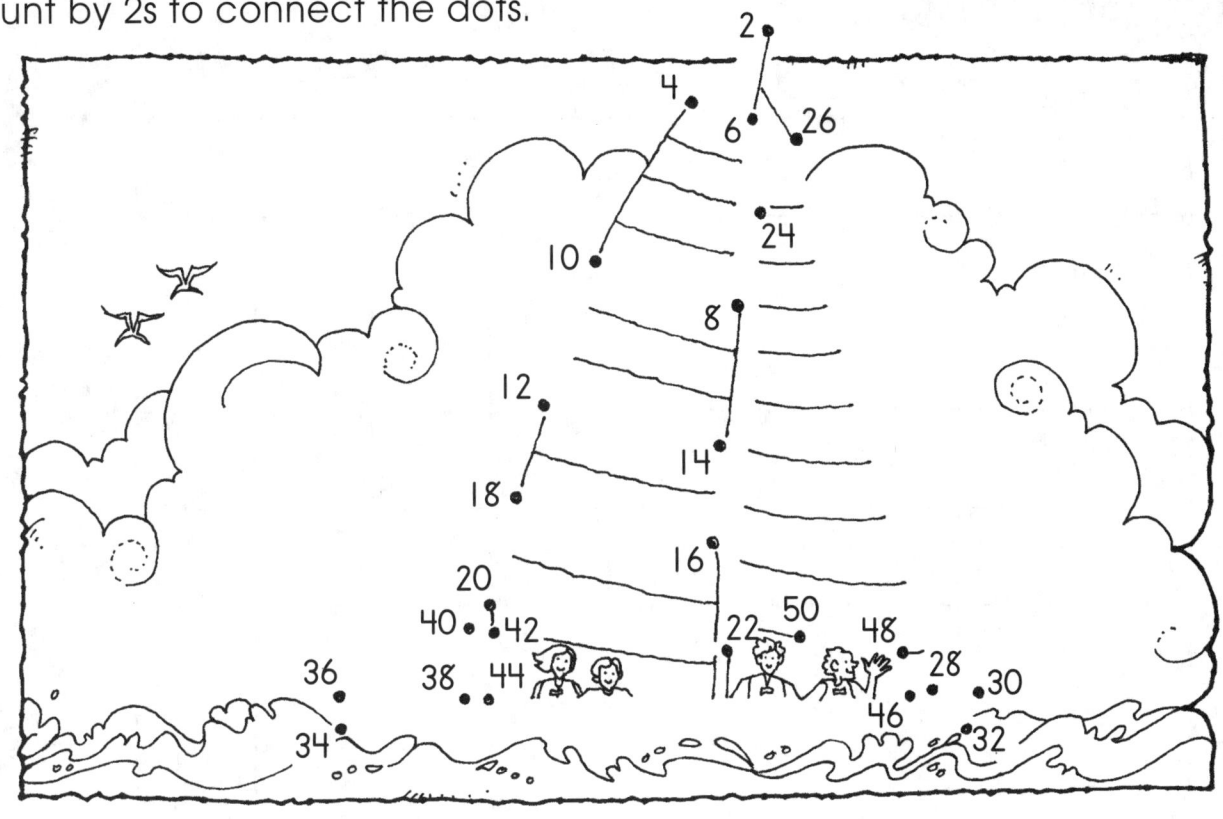

Fill in the missing numbers.

5 _____ 15 _____ 25 _____ _____ 40 _____ _____

55 _____ 65 _____ _____ _____ _____ _____

Draw a line to match each number word with the correct numeral.

ten   twenty   thirty   forty   fifty

20   60   10   50   70   40   80   100   30   90

sixty   seventy   eighty   ninety   one hundred

Sunny Sums

addition and subtraction

Fill in the addition chart.

+	1	2	3	4	5	6	7	8	9
1									
2									
3									
4									
5									
6									
7									
8									
9									

Explain how you can use the addition chart to figure out subtraction facts.

_____

_____

Use the chart to make addition and subtraction flash cards. Use blank index cards. Practice your facts. Write the problem on one side and the answer on the other side.

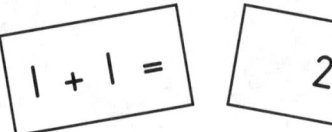

Daily Double

doubles facts

Complete the picture to help you solve each doubles fact.

A. Draw dots on the dice.

5 + 5 = ____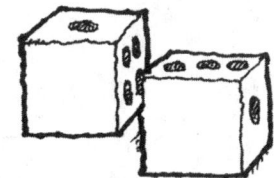

B. Draw petals on the flowers.

7 + 7 = ____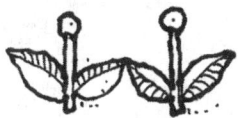

C. Draw spots on the ladybugs.

2 + 2 = ____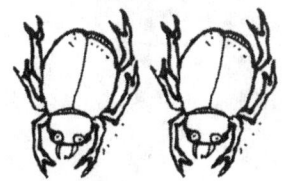

D. Draw hearts on the T-shirts.

9 + 9 = ____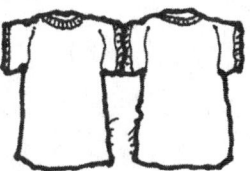

E. Draw legs on the spiders.

8 + 8 = ____

F. Draw kids on the buses.

3 + 3 = ____

G. Draw eggs in the nests.

6 + 6 = ____

H. Draw wings on the butterflies.

4 + 4 = ____

Write two addition facts and two subtraction facts for each picture.

I.

___ + ___ = ____

___ + ___ = ____

___ − ___ = ____

___ − ___ = ____

J.

___ + ___ = ____

___ + ___ = ____

___ − ___ = ____

___ − ___ = ____

K.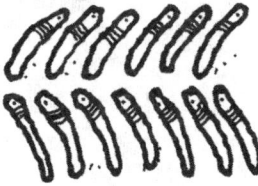

___ + ___ = ____

___ + ___ = ____

___ + ___ = ____

___ + ___ = ____

CD-0264 Set Sail for Summer

© Carson-Dellosa

Make It Ten

addition and subtraction

When adding and subtracting numbers greater than 10, it is helpful to think first about "what makes 10."

Examples: 6 + 5   14 – 5
Think: 6 + 4 + 1   Think: 14 – 4 – 1

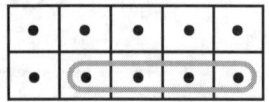   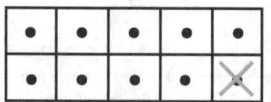 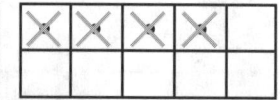

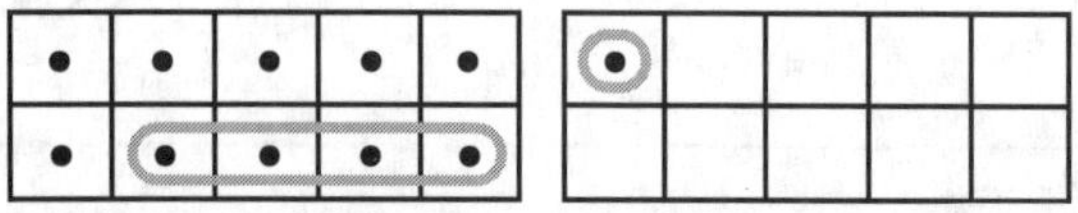

Add 4 to make 10. One more makes 11.   Take away 4 to make 10.
Take 1 more to leave 9.

Solve. Use the 10 frames at the bottom of the page to help you.

A. 11 – 3 = _____   I. 5 + 9 = _____   Q. 8 + 5 = _____

B. 11 – 2 = _____   J. 6 + 8 = _____   R. 7 + 8 = _____

C. 8 + 9 = _____   K. 18 – 9 = _____   S. 14 – 9 = _____

D. 14 – 6 = _____   L. 12 – 4 = _____   T. 13 – 4 = _____

E. 9 + 7 = _____   M. 8 + 3 = _____   U. 9 + 4 = _____

F. 9 + 3 = _____   N. 15 – 6 = _____   V. 12 – 3 = _____

G. 17 – 9 = _____   O. 13 – 5 = _____   W. 15 – 7 = _____

H. 9 + 2 = _____   P. 17 – 8 = _____   X. 16 – 8 = _____

© Carson-Dellosa   22   CD-0264 *Set Sail for Summer*

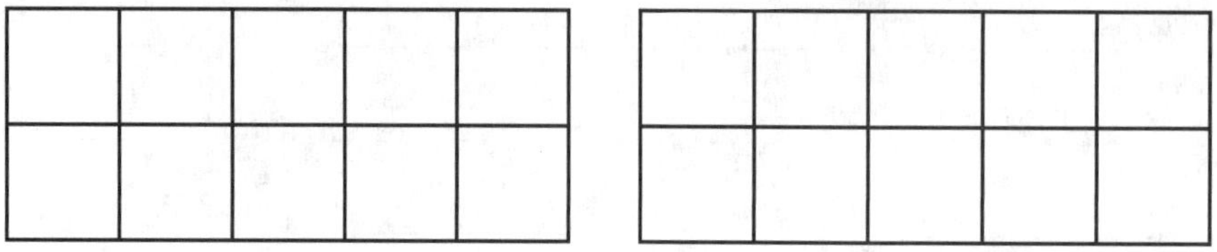

Knock, Knock Joke

two-digit addition and subtraction

Solve the equations. Then, write the correct word above each answer below to uncover a joke.

A. 10 + 15 owl	B. 42 + 27 the	C. 47 + 31 who	D. 37 − 16 who's
E. 87 − 35 knock	F. 23 + 24 know	G. 53 + 23 open	H. 44 + 44 unless
I. 20 − 4 there	J. 25 − 10 door	K. 65 − 34 you	

_____ , _____ .
   52   52

_____ ?
   21   16

_____ .
   25

_____ ?
   25   78

_____ _____ _____ _____
   25   31   47   88

_____ ?
   31   76   69   15

Building Blocks

graphing/geometry

Count the geometric blocks and record the data in the graph.

Geometric Blocks

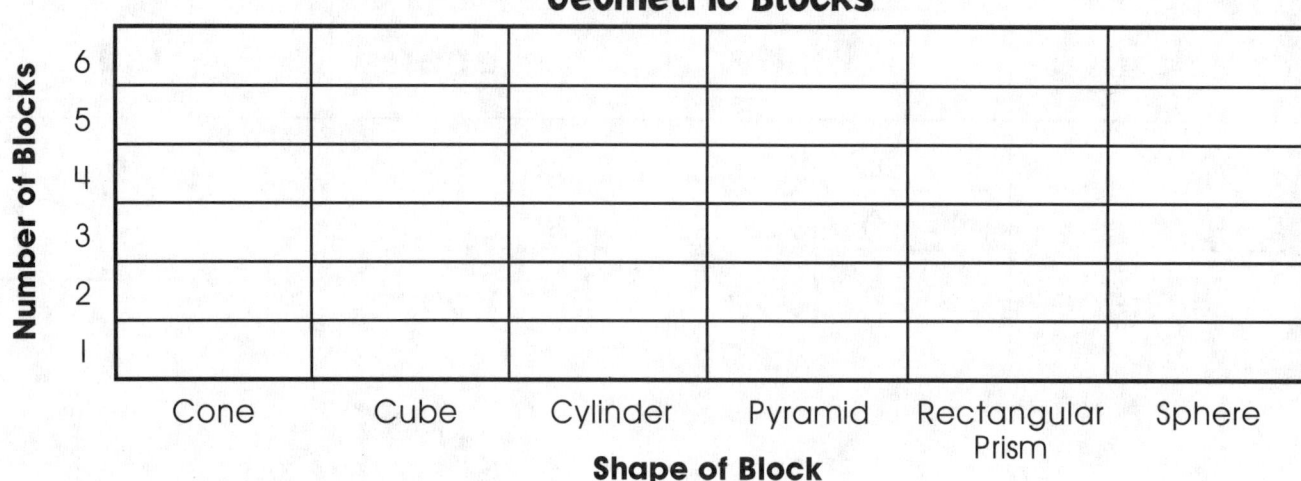

Use your graph to answer the questions.

1. How many more cubes than rectangular prisms? _____
2. How many fewer cones than cylinders? _____
3. Of which two shapes are there the same number? _____ _____
4. How many blocks are there in all? _____
5. How many blocks have six faces? _____
6. How many more spheres than pyramids? _____

Challenge: Find things in or around your home that are the same shapes as the blocks above. Make another graph of what you find.

© Carson-Dellosa   24   CD-0264 Set Sail for Summer

Measuring at Home

measurement

Use a ruler to measure each item. Record whether you are using inches, feet, centimeters, or meters. Number the items in order of length.

1. height of a video 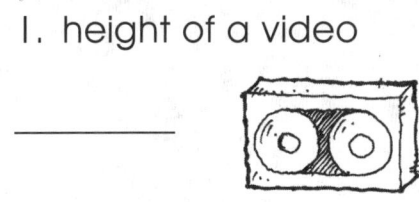	2. length of a bed 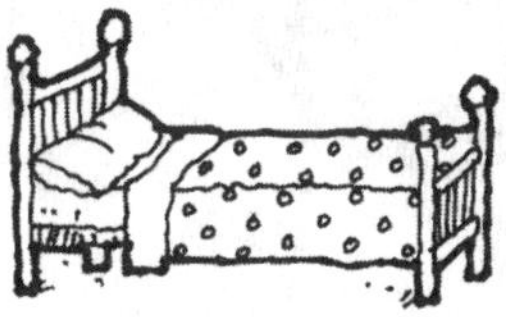 	3. length of a shoe 
_____	_____	_____

Measure the circumference of these items with a string. Then, measure the string. Record the units used. Number the items in order of circumference.

4. apple	5. lamp shade	6. ball
_____	_____	_____

Use a measuring cup to measure the volume of each container. Record the units used. Number the items in order of volume.

7. saucepan	8. cereal bowl	9. drinking glass
_____	_____	_____

Weigh yourself on a scale. Pick up each item and step on the scale again. Subtract your weight to find each measurement. Record the units used. Number the items in order of weight.

10. chair	11. bag of 10 books	12. pair of shoes
_____	_____	_____

CD-0264 *Set Sail for Summer*   25   © Carson-Dellosa

Got the Time?

time

Write the time below each clock.

1.  2.  3.  4.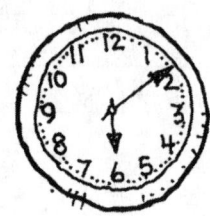

_____   _____   _____   _____

Draw the hands to show the correct time on each clock.

5. 6:30   6. 12:03   7. 2:50   8. 4:19

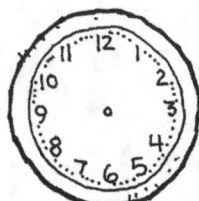   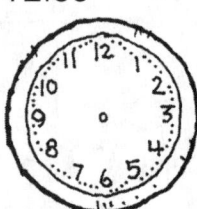      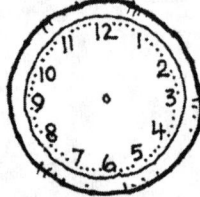

Write the day of the week that comes before or after.

9. _____ Monday   10. Thursday _____

11. _____ Sunday   12. Tuesday _____

13. Sunday _____   14. _____ Wednesday

Write the month that comes before or after.

15. September _____   16. May _____

17. November _____   18. _____ March

19. July _____   20. _____ April

Challenge: Look at a clock in your house. Record the exact time. _____
Walk away and do something else for five minutes. Come back
when you think the five minutes are up. Record the time again. _____
How close were you? Try again.

© Carson-Dellosa   26   CD-0264 *Set Sail for Summer*

Lemonade Stand

money

Look at the coins given. Color the fewest coins needed for each purchase.

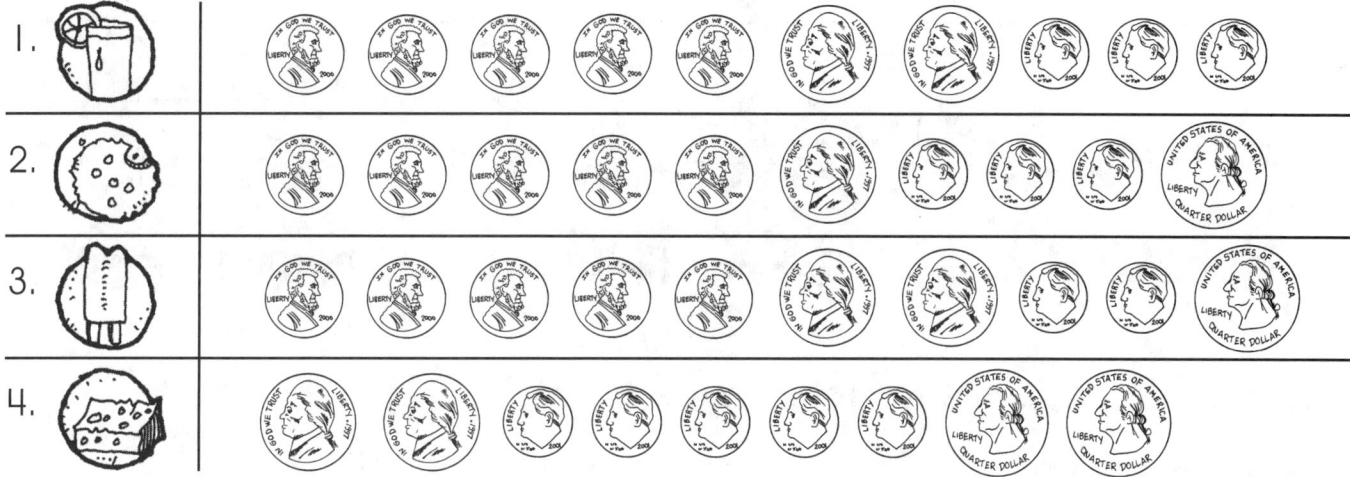

How much would it cost?

5. 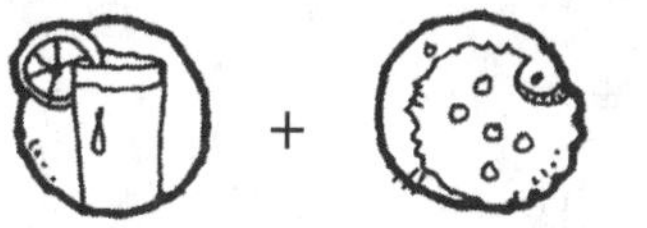 🥤 + 🍪 _____

6. 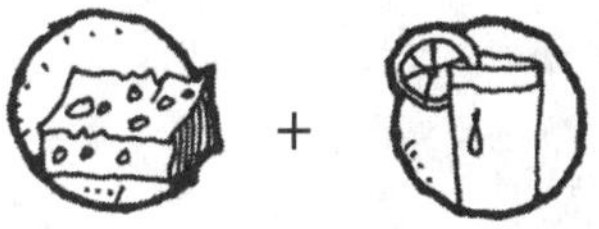 🍰 + 🥤 _____

7. 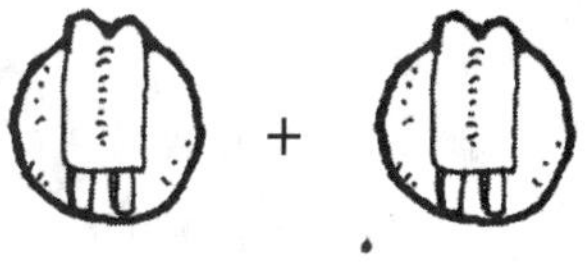 🍦 + 🍦 _____

What would be your change?

8. You give 3 dimes for a glass of lemonade. _____

9. You give 2 quarters for a cookie. _____

10. You give 2 quarters for an ice-cream bar. _____

11. You give 3 quarters and 3 dimes for a brownie. _____

Challenge: Use real money to show the amount needed to buy each item. Use different coins than the ones you used above. Draw the coins you used.

CD-0264 *Set Sail for Summer*   27   © Carson-Dellosa

Twos and Threes

multiplication

Count how many. Write the total on the line.

A. 2 x 2 = ____

B. 2 x 3 = ____

C. 2 x 5 = ____
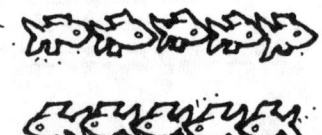

D. 2 x 6 = ____

E. 2 x 7 = ____
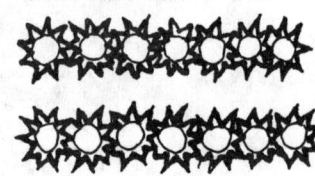

F. 2 x 8 = ____
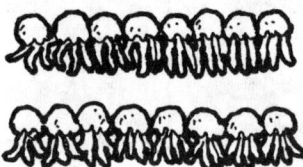

Count how many. Write the total on the line.

G. How many eggs?

3 x 2 = ____

H. How many wheels?

3 x 4 = ____

I. How many petals?

3 x 5 = ____

J. How many stars?

3 x 6 = ____

K. How many grapes?

3 x 7 = ____
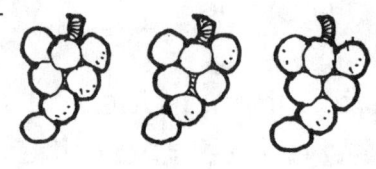

L. How many leaves?

3 x 9 = ____

Number Stories

problem solving

Read the stories carefully and solve. Draw a picture if it helps.

1. Serena had some frozen juice bars. She gave 5 to her friends and had 7 left. How many did she start with?

   _____

2. Adam and his sister have 20 videos. If 8 of the videos are his sister's, how many are Adam's?

   _____

3. Raffi has 8 leaves in his collection. Keisha has 17 in her collection. How many fewer leaves does Raffi have?

   _____

4. Peter played basketball for 4 hours on Monday. He played 2 hours longer than that on Tuesday. How many hours total did he play on those 2 days?

   _____

5. Javier has $15 in his bank. Ben has $9 in his. What is the difference in the amount they have saved?

   _____

6. Seventeen kids are swimming in the pool. There are 3 more boys than girls. How many boys are swimming?

   _____

7. At the park, 2 girls are playing on the swings, 8 are playing soccer, and 4 are jumping rope. How many girls are playing at the park?

   _____

8. It is Sam's birthday. His brother Luka is 14 years old. Luka was 4 when Sam was born. How old is Sam?

   _____

CD-0264 Set Sail for Summer   29   © Carson-Dellosa

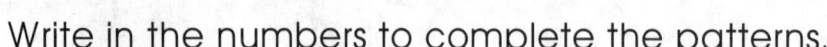

Number Patterns

problem solving

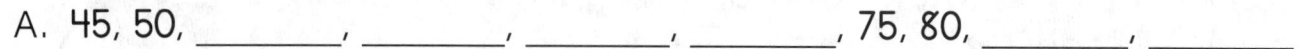

Write in the numbers to complete the patterns.

A. 45, 50, _____, _____, _____, 75, 80, _____, _____

B. 60, 55, _____, 45, _____, _____, _____, 25, _____, _____, 10

C. 2, 4, _____, 8, _____, 12, _____, _____, _____, 20, _____

D. 81, _____, _____, _____, 85, _____, _____, _____, 89

E. 32, _____, 36, _____, 40, _____, _____, _____, 48, _____

F. 33, 33, 34, _____, _____, 35, _____, _____, 37, 37, _____, 38

G. 99, _____, 97, _____, _____, 94, _____, _____, _____, 90

H. 280, 270, _____, _____, _____, 230, _____, _____, 200

I. 3, 6, 9, _____, 15, _____, 21, _____, _____, _____, _____

Challenge: 10, 15, 13, 18, 16, _____, _____, 24, _____, 27, _____

© Carson-Dellosa

CD-0264 *Set Sail for Summer*

Around the World

map skills

Name the seven continents and four oceans shown on the map. Write the correct letter next to each name.

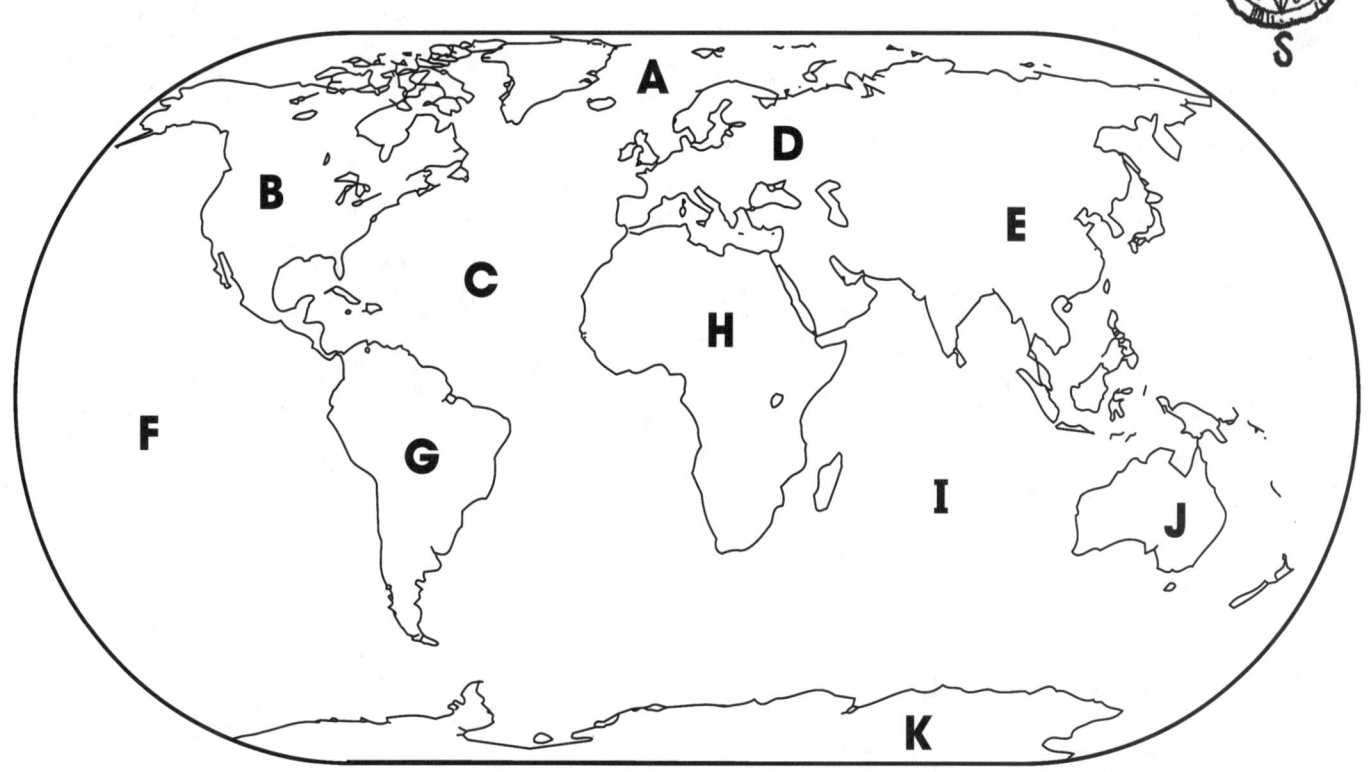

____ Africa   ____ Europe   ____ Atlantic Ocean

____ Antarctica   ____ North America   ____ Indian Ocean

____ Asia   ____ South America   ____ Pacific Ocean

____ Australia   ____ Arctic Ocean

Challenge: Do you know people or have friends who are from other countries? Look in an atlas or at a detailed world map to find their native countries. Learn something about those countries. Draw their flags.

Answer Key

p. 8—The Three Bears
1. three bears and a boy
2. long ago in a castle far away
3. pancakes are too hot
4. Baby Bear was lonely
5. The boy and Baby Bear became friends.
6. "once upon a time," three, live in a castle, the bears can talk, they live happily ever after

p. 9—What's Next?
1. b   2. a   3. c
4. a   5. b   6. a

p. 11—Insects

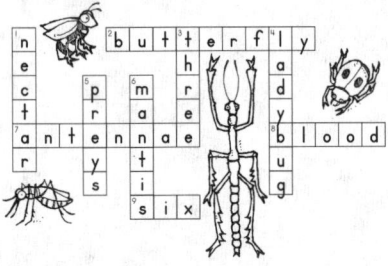

p. 12—Camping Trip
Francisco forgot his shoes and pillow. Ben forgot his toothbrush and sweatshirt.
1. shoes, socks, toothbrush, pillow, sleeping bag, sweatshirt, T-shirts
2. pajamas, jeans, book
3. shorts, toothpaste, radio
4. Francisco, book; Ben, radio

p. 13—Alphabet Adventure
Stories will vary but elements should follow alphabetical order.

p. 14—ABC Ice Cream
A. 3   B. 3   C. 3   D. 3
   2   2   4   1
   4   1   2   4
   1   4   1   2

E. 1   F. 2   Challenge: There
   3   1   are six possible
   4   4   combinations.
   2   3   Nine if you
              flip the order.

p. 15—Summer Analogies
1. snowy or cold day
2. river or lake
3. pea, corn, tomato (Answers will vary.)
4. skates
5. sailboat
6. rain
7. air or tree
8. eyes or face

p. 16—Phoebe's Vacation

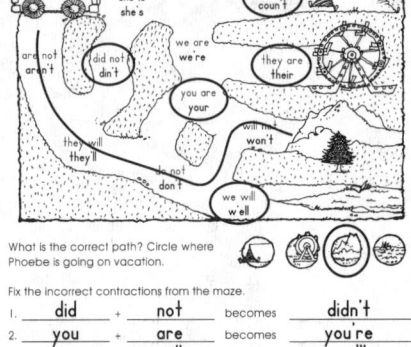

Fix the incorrect contractions from the maze.
1. did + not becomes didn't
2. you + are becomes you're
3. we + will becomes we'll
4. they + are becomes they're
5. could + not becomes couldn't

p. 17—Park Play
Pictures will vary but should follow the directions given.
2. There are 5 squirrels.
3. The cow and giraffe should be circled.
4. The child is dressed for a cold winter day.

p. 18—Beach Bash
Answers will vary.
1. buddy, pal
2. shout, scream
3. lovely, beautiful
4. nasty, unkind
5. friendly, kind
6. large, huge
7. cap, hood
8. lad, guy
9. sack, pack
10. enemy
11. whisper
12. ugly
13. nice
14. little
15. girl

p. 19—Summer Sailing

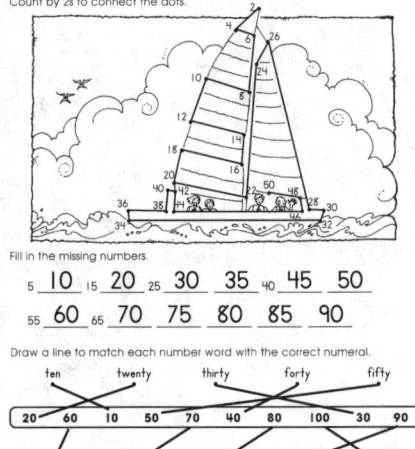

Fill in the missing numbers.
5 10 15 20 25 30 35 40 45 50
55 60 65 70 75 80 85 90

Draw a line to match each number word with the correct numeral.
ten — 10
twenty — 20
thirty — 30
forty — 40
fifty — 50
sixty — 60
seventy — 70
eighty — 80
ninety — 90
one hundred — 100

p. 20—Sunny Sums

+	1	2	3	4	5	6	7	8	9
1	2	3	4	5	6	7	8	9	10
2	3	4	5	6	7	8	9	10	11
3	4	5	6	7	8	9	10	11	12
4	5	6	7	8	9	10	11	12	13
5	6	7	8	9	10	11	12	13	14
6	7	8	9	10	11	12	13	14	15
7	8	9	10	11	12	13	14	15	16
8	9	10	11	12	13	14	15	16	17
9	10	11	12	13	14	15	16	17	18

To use the chart for subtraction facts, begin by pointing to a box in the grid. Use your other finger to slide all the way over to the left. This is the number you are subtracting from the first number. Slide the first finger up to find the difference.

© Carson-Dellosa